Choosing Wisely in Life

7 Steps to a Quality Decision

by
Dr. Buddy Harrison

Harrison House
Tulsa, Oklahoma

Unless otherwise indicated, all Scripture quotations are taken from the *King James Version* of the Bible.

Scripture quotations marked NKJV are taken from *The New King James Version*. Copyright © 1979, 1980, 1982, Thomas Nelson, Inc.

Cover photo by Richard Foster
Tulsa, Oklahoma

07 06 05 04   10 9 8 7 6 5 4 3 2 1

Choosing Wisely in Life:
7 Steps to a Quality Decision
ISBN 1-57794-104-7
Copyright © 2003, 2004 by Patsy G. Harrison. Revised.
P.O. Box 35443
Tulsa, Oklahoma 74153

Previously published as *7 Steps to a Quality Decision*
ISBN 0-89274-736-6
Copyright © 1996 by Buddy Harrison

Published by Harrison House, Inc.
P.O. Box 35035
Tulsa, Oklahoma 74153

CONTENTS

1

GOD'S PATTERN FOR MAKING DECISIONS

God never intended us to operate haphazardly. He does not operate that way. And He certainly does not expect us to operate that way either.

We know how special we are to God because He gave us freedom of choice. Since God created us to make decisions, we can be sure that He has also given us the proper way to make those decisions. He will show us what to do and how to do it.

God gave us His Word, the Bible, as a model and a guide for how we are to conduct our lives. And that is where we find a pattern for decision making. The pattern applies to "natural" decisions as well as "spiritual" decisions. These are the seven steps necessary to "choosing wisely."

The following Scriptures contain the outline of godly decision making. Read them very carefully because we are going to return to these words frequently. And pay special attention to the seven italicized words:

> By faith Moses, when he was come to years, *refused* to be called the son of Pharaoh's daughter; *choosing* rather to suffer affliction with the people of God, than to enjoy the pleasures of sin for a season; *esteeming* the reproach of Christ greater riches than the treasures in Egypt: for he had respect unto the recompence of the reward.
>
> By faith he *forsook* Egypt, not fearing the wrath of the king: for he *endured* as seeing him who is invisible. Through faith he *kept* the passover, and the sprinkling of blood, lest he that destroyed the firstborn should touch them. By faith they *passed through* the Red sea as by dry land: which the Egyptians assaying to do were drowned.
>
> Hebrews 11:24-29

This passage shows us seven steps that Moses took in deciding to lead God's people out of Egypt. We will see how Moses weighed the options and arrived at his decision. Then we will study the essential "action steps" that he took in fulfilling the direction that God had given him.

As you study this process, you will see the pattern for making decisions in your life. Most importantly, you will learn the seven steps necessary to complete this godly decision-making process. Many people only get to a point of *mental assent* in the decision-making process. In other words, a person can have a strong desire to do something and believe in his mind that he has made a decision to do it, but never get around to actually doing it. He never follows through; he never makes it happen. (How many times in the past have you made a resolution to accomplish a certain goal or to change a behavior only to have it slip away?) But by learning the procedures and rules that God teaches, you will understand how to make quality choices and decisions. And you will learn how to *act* upon your decisions to achieve the desires, goals, plans, and dreams that God has given you.

The first three steps in the decision-making process, *esteeming, choosing, and refusing,* are made by your heart or by your mind, depending on whether the decision is spiritual or natural. So these first three steps are called "heart steps" or "mental steps," depending on the character of the decision. (The last four steps are called "action steps" and will be discussed later.) Since your head (your mind) is also involved in spiritual decisions, I will refer to the first three steps as the head steps or the mental steps. Natural decisions will affect matters that you can see, feel, taste, touch, or smell. Spiritual decisions are those that are controlled by your spirit, your "inward man."

Sometimes people put off making decisions believing that they have not "heard from God." *If the Lord has not spoken to you after you have prayed about a situation, you can still make a decision with your head!* God's grace abounds! He will help you overcome.

God's Timing

Before we look at the steps involved, notice in our text the phrase "by faith Moses, when he was *come to years.*" One of the greatest hindrances to quality decisions is the pressure to hurry. One of the most important things to learn about making quality decisions is *to not get in a hurry*. Any time you get that old hurry-up feeling, look out! You are about to get in trouble. The devil is trying to force the issue, trying to get you to act before you have gone through all of the essential steps to make the right decision.

This phrase "come to years" means that the proper time had come for Moses to take action — the timing was right. If God has told you He has a certain thing for you to do, that does not necessarily mean that you should begin doing it that very moment. Often, time is needed to prepare our hearts as well as our minds and bodies. If we are not careful about the timing, we might not accomplish what God wants us to do.

A number of years ago during one of Kenneth Hagin's crusades I was caught up into the spiritual realm. God began to speak to me about certain things that would happen in my life and ministry. It took more than ten years for those things to come into being. Yet I have seen certain people mess up their lives and their ministries by failing to be sensitive to the *timing* of the Lord. Their minds are like cement, thoroughly mixed and well set! Some miss God by failing to lay a solid foundation. Others get out ahead of God and discover that the people to minister to are not yet ready to receive. When the Lord speaks to you about things that He desires for you to do, do not let your enthusiasm and zeal cause you to run off unprepared. Do not take off at the wrong time, or you will miss what God has for you to do. Remember, God is a God of order and timing.

Moses was not always in God's timing. As a young man he became anxious. He saw an Egyptian beating one of the Hebrew slaves, and without thinking he killed the Egyptian and hid the body. (Ex. 2:11,12.) Moses knew that he was God's man, that he was called to deliver God's people. But his timing was off by about forty years. He acted before the Spirit of God told him to and made a mess of things.

As the deliverer of the children of Israel, Moses was a type and shadow of Jesus Christ, our Deliverer. But Jesus never missed God's timing. Notice that Jesus waited until He was thirty years old, when he had "come to years," before he even began His ministry. The devil will use any tool available — your age, your race, your background, your pride — to try to get you to hurry up and mess up.

Certainly I do not mean that you should procrastinate and put off doing what you know God has called you to do. Sometimes things will happen much more quickly than you ever thought possible. But do not be discouraged if matters in your life seem to be taking longer than you would like. Do not run ahead of God. Until you have sufficient training, you will not be able to fight the good fight of faith as effectively as you would like. In the past I have hurried and made a mess of things. I have since learned not to rush. You do not have to beat your brains out or get involved in a big promotional program so that you can be on God's timetable. Learn to wait on the Lord and on His timing.

As you go through these chapters, begin to compare the way you have made decisions in the past with God's pattern for decision making. As you learn these seven steps and begin to make decisions God's way, your life will never be the same!

2

WEIGHING THE CHOICES

Esteeming the reproach of Christ greater riches
than the treasures in Egypt: for he had respect
unto the recompence of the reward.

Hebrews 11:26

The first three steps in making a quality decision,
the "heart" or "mental" steps (depending on whether
the decision is spiritual or natural), are intertwined
and woven together. To understand these important
steps, imagine a seesaw on a playground or picture
the scales in the old grocery stores that were used to
weigh merchandise. Both the scales and the seesaw
have a balance point in the center. If the objects on
both sides weigh the same, the two sides will balance.
If one side is heavier, that side will go down and the
other side will go up.

In making a quality decision, you must determine the weight, or value, you will give to the objects you are choosing between. Only after doing that can you decide between the choices. Only then can you intelligently *refuse* and *choose* the different options you have. This process of giving weight (or value) to those objects is called "esteeming." This is the first step and the controlling factor in making a quality decision.

Esteeming the Situation

The most common meaning of *esteem* is to honor, to hold something or someone in high regard.[1] But esteem in the sense I am using it here means to judge, to weigh, to balance, to measure, to add up or give an account.[2]

Many times people will make important decisions without judging the options, without weighing the positives and negatives, without measuring the alternatives, without determining how that decision will add up in the long run. They are not *esteeming* the situation.

This process goes on all the time even when we might not be aware of it. Consider, for example, a woman buying a pair of shoes. Her decision to purchase a particular pair of shoes will result from determining what is important to her. Depending on the situation, the determining factor might be color, comfort, or style. She might be looking for a color to wear with a particular outfit. If she finds shoes in the correct color, she may buy them even if the fit bothers her a little. Or she may be looking for high heels for a formal occasion. She might try on a pair of shoes that are very comfortable but have low heels. No matter how comfortable they may be, she will tell the clerk, "No, that's not what I want." Even in this ordinary, routine action, she is esteeming the situation.

Choosing Between What You Want To Do and What You Ought To Do

It is not difficult to make a decision if one choice greatly outweighs the other. But sometimes each of the choices has great value, and you have to choose between them. God said to Moses, "Come now therefore, and I will send thee unto Pharaoh, that thou mayest bring forth my people the children of Israel out of Egypt" (Ex. 3:10). Moses esteemed the situation. He put the choices he had to make in the balance. He weighed the reproach of Christ and found it to be greater riches (of greater value) than the treasures of Egypt.

Just because you know what you should do does not make it easy. And certainly this was not a simple decision for Moses to make. As "The Son of Pharaoh's Daughter," Moses held a position of great wealth and power. He was in the royal line and entitled to an inheritance. Probably he would become king himself some day. He had to decide whether he would be a king of Egypt or a king in heaven.

Your Title and Position With God

Have you ever had to consider giving something up — something that you knew you should give up — then you began to think about how much you liked that thing, or how hard you had worked for it, or how long it had taken you to get in that position? But we have to choose between having our position and title in the natural world and our position and title with God. Moses determined that the reproach of Christ was worth more than any earthly treasures he would receive if he stayed in Egypt. I will tell you this, if you go after your heavenly Father, you will have a title, you will have position, you will have wealth. And spiritual blessings are going to *overtake* you.

Valuing God's Word

Until you value God's Word as it affects your choices, you will not be able to make quality, godly decisions. Some people esteem the Word highly. They feed upon it, treasure it, and keep it in their hearts, allowing it to become a part of their lives. Consequently, the Word of God and the Spirit of God mean more to them than life itself. But others treat the Word as just another book. It is a shame that they hold God's Word in such low esteem. They might say they believe that the Bible is God's Word, but they do not "esteem" it. It has no value, depth, or meaning to them. In the same way, many believers hold the gifts of the Holy Ghost in low esteem. Because they do not value the gifts, they will never gain any benefit from them.

Everything, from canned goods at the grocery store to gold and diamonds, is weighed to establish its value. And whether we are aware of doing so or not, we weigh the various choices we have as we determine which ones to make.

We also give weight, or value, to spiritual matters. This is reflected by our actions or lack of actions. For example, you might believe that God is in the healing business and that His desire is that everyone walks in perfect health. But how you act when sickness occurs in your life will indicate the esteem you have for God's promise. God promises you strength, vitality, and a long life. (Eph. 6:3; Prov. 4:22; Ps. 103:1-5.) If you esteem and value this promise, then you will be able to resist the reproach and criticism of those who do not believe in healing. By placing value on God's supernatural power, you place yourself in a position to receive the benefit of that power. The more you look in the Word, the more you will find how powerful that Word is in your life.

How do you esteem tithing? Has it become an important part of your spiritual life, or do you consider it to be insignificant — or maybe even a bother? You may *believe* in tithing and yet find yourself debating whether you should give your tithe to the Lord this week. If you view tithing as having to pay 10 percent of your income to God and you think you do not have enough as it is, then you will not give much value to tithing. But if you understand the value that God places on tithing, if you understand that tithing is the foundation of God's plan for great prosperity in your life, then you will get excited about tithing. As you place great value on the promises that God has made to those who tithe and are faithful to follow His command, you will expect God to do what He promised: "open you the windows of heaven, and pour you out a blessing, that there shall not be room enough to receive it" (Mal. 3:10).

Building on the Rock

The more you rely on and build trust in God, the more you will establish a stockpile of experiences that you can draw from in the future. When I was working as a manager of a Dairy Queen, I began to think about entering the ministry full time. I was given an opportunity to go to Minnesota as a Music and Youth Director, and about the same time was approached with a very tempting business deal. My boss offered me a position as manager of *three* of the Dairy Queen stores. If I took the offer, he would give me a substantial increase in salary, and the salary would continue to increase for two more years. After that I would have an opportunity to buy part of the business. That was good money, especially since I did not have a college education at that time, and it was not an easy decision to make.

But an experience years before helped me enormously in making the choice between these two opportunities.

When I was a young man I went to my pastor, Brother Leonard Wood of the First Assembly of God in Garland, Texas, and told him that I wanted to "do something for God." I offered to clean the church or mow the yard, to do anything to help. But Brother Wood told me he already had people to do that work and instead asked me to start a choir. That is not what I had in mind. I had no formal training in this area. I could not even read music. I could sing and I had a good ear, which means I could tell when someone was singing the wrong note. But I could not tell someone else what note to sing, only whether to go up or down! My natural feeling told me that I had nothing to offer, but because I esteemed the wisdom of my pastor and knew that he would not ask me to do something that I could not do, I agreed to try.

I prayed that God would help me overcome my lack of knowledge and inexperience, and I took on the job of starting a choir with a mixture of uneasiness and enthusiasm. During rehearsals we would fish for a note until we had it, and we kept working at it until we would get the harmony. Not only did the music come together, God's Spirit began to move in our choir rehearsals. Teenagers were saved, others were filled with the Holy Ghost, and the gifts of the Spirit began to operate during practice. These were not your ordinary, everyday choir practices. You see, I had placed great value upon serving God, and God honored me in return.

One evening during a service one of the members of the choir, a boy named Bob, sang the old song "I'll Meet You in the Morning." You could almost reach out and touch the anointing on his singing. It seemed like it came down and stayed with us as we returned to the choir room to hang up our robes. I looked at

Bob and said, "I love you, man!" At that moment everyone became quiet and still. Then praises to God started to rise like a musical crescendo. A young Methodist girl who was visiting raised her hands in praise and began speaking in tongues as she was filled with the Holy Spirit. The power of God swept through the room. Teenagers were crying, laughing, and praying in the Spirit all at the same time.

I became concerned that the excitement and commotion in the choir room would disturb the church service. Hurriedly re-entering the sanctuary through the side door I whispered to the pastor, "Brother Wood, something has happened in there, and *I didn't start it!*" He smiled at me and said, "I know it, I know it; now bring it out here!"

Now what am I going to do? I thought to myself, *How am I going to get that in there out here to the sanctuary?* I knew what was happening in the choir room was spiritual — that it was from the Lord — still I knew of no way to walk in the choir room and pick up the Holy Ghost! But again I believed that my pastor would not ask me to do something that was not possible, so I returned to the choir room.

As I entered, I saw the pastor's nephew, Jimmy D., standing with his eyes closed and his hands raised, singing in the spirit and worshipping the Lord. It was as though he and Jesus were standing miles away from anyone else. Since obviously he was filled with what Pastor Wood had told me to bring back, I simply nudged Jimmy D. through the side door back into the auditorium. Still worshipping the Lord, he walked through the church. He reached over and laid his hand on a teenager who immediately ran to the altar to be saved. At the same time other teenagers piled out of the choir room and started praying and laying hands on members of the congregation who also ran to the altar. Four were saved that night; thirteen were filled with the Spirit.

Draw on Your Past Experiences

Now as I was faced with choosing between a promotion with Dairy Queen and going into full-time ministry, choosing between thousands of dollars in increased salary and going to another place where I *still* could not read music, I was able to draw upon my past experience. I knew that I had reached a place where I valued and treasured God's promise to provide for me, a place where I could rely on my trust in God and not be led astray by fear of my own inadequacy, a place where I was more excited about what God would help me accomplish than the comfort that extra money might provide.

Becoming All You Can Be

The things you value determine your course in life. Moses esteemed the reproach of Christ as greater than all the riches in Egypt. As you learn to judge, to weigh, to balance, to measure, to value, to *esteem* the choices presented to you, more than ever before you will find yourself willing to give up temporary comforts and pleasures so that you can achieve what God has planned for your life.

3

CHOOSE AND REFUSE:
HOW PRIORITIES ARE CREATED

By faith Moses, when he was come to years,
refused to be called the son of Pharaoh's
daughter; *choosing* rather to suffer affliction
with the people of God, than to enjoy
the pleasures of sin for a season.

Hebrews 11:24,25

After *esteeming* your options, you are now faced with the essential and major responsibility of setting priorities. Some options are not good for us and need to be rejected. Others may seem good but are not in the path that God wants us to walk. What do we choose? What do we refuse?

Refuse means to deny, to denounce, to reject, to disown.[3] You can do that by your words and by your life. We refuse that which we perceive to be negative or of lesser value.

Choose means to select or to pick out.[4] We choose that which we perceive to be of greater worth, the positive option.

Notice that when we initially make the decision in our minds, nothing has actually been *done*. We may call it a decision, but it still is not a *quality* decision.

Moses refused to be called the son of Pharaoh's daughter. What does that mean? What was he refusing? By renouncing the title, "Son of Pharaoh's Daughter," Moses forfeited all of his rights and power in Egypt. Similar to a king abdicating his throne, he relinquished all of his wealth and all that he was due from his station in life: the money, the land, the servants, the trips abroad.

At the same time Moses *chose* "to suffer affliction with the people rather than to enjoy the pleasures of sin for a season." Be careful here. Some people really get into "suffering affliction" for the Lord, even when He does not want them to suffer. Moses knew that the pleasures of sin lasted only for a season, and that the things of God are eternal. God's principles and precepts never change. But do not focus on affliction right now. Instead I want you to see a very simple spiritual principle. *There must be a willingness on your part to choose what God would have you do.* "Seek ye first the kingdom of God, and his righteousness; and all these things shall be added unto you" (Matt. 6:33). That is when the other things that you desire will come along.

The "natural man" believes with his carnal mind that it is too hard to make a commitment that might require him to give up pleasure or friends or money. All those "things" seem so important, so central to his existence. In fact, many people *fear* that God will take things from them if they commit to Him. But suddenly, when that person becomes a new creature in Christ, there is a new thrust, a new drive behind him. He now has a relationship with God. And *all* those things that are really good for him and that will really make him happy are in the process of being added to him.

If you get your eyes on your bills and on your problems, you will neither see God nor seek Him. I love my children *because* they are my children, not out of any sense of obligation nor any thought of what they might do for me. My love springs from relationship, not duty. And our relationship to God is exactly the same. He loves us because of *who we are,* His children, and He *wants* to bless us.

As you keep your eyes on Him, the blessings of God are going to overtake you. The finances will come; the bills will be paid. Keep choosing relationship and fellowship with God, and refuse the doubt and worry that is so destructive.

Years ago my wife, Pat, and I made a quality decision to work for her father, Kenneth Hagin — for the grand, glorious, and total sum of fifty dollars a week. For both of us!

As early as my courtship days with Pat, my family already had a problem with the relationship — because of the potential relatives! Of course, they knew that Pat was nice and sweet and pretty. But they didn't understand her father's methods. To tell the truth, I didn't either! But I wanted to marry his daughter, not his methods.

Now there was a new problem. My family had heard that Hagin had been referred to as a "Prophet of God." For them, that was just too much. It was plain to them that prophets existed only in Bible times, and they made it just as plain to me that my working for Kenneth Hagin would create a barrier between us. In other words, they forced me to choose between associating with his ministry or associating with them.

You know, some things can be given up pretty easily. But giving up an entire family is not one of them. It was not my idea, but they had drawn the line in the sand.

I had watched Brother Hagin closely for quite a while. I knew that he was teaching and preaching truth. And I knew the Bible says, "He that receiveth a prophet in the name of a prophet shall receive a prophet's reward" (Matt. 10:41). I placed greater weight and value upon what I had seen and observed in Brother Hagin than on the negative lifestyle and opinions of my own family. Besides, following God was more important to me than the salary I would receive.

Despite the intimidation of my family, I followed the man of God. And I learned a great lesson in the process. Even though some decisions are a little hard on the flesh, every situation that God has called me to has been good — *every single time!* When I refuse the mediocre and choose excellence, when I love God and purpose to follow Him wherever He leads, His blessings just overtake me.

At one time, my daughter Candas had a tendency to think and speak very negatively. Frequently she would express anything that went through her mind without really thinking about what she was saying. We have to be careful about the words we choose and the words we refuse. We even have to learn which *thoughts* we will accept and which ones we will reject, "casting down imaginations, and every high thing that exalteth itself against the knowledge of God, and bringing into captivity *every thought* to the obedience of Christ" (2 Cor. 10:5).

During this same time frame, Candas seemed to enjoy her "pity parties." Proverbs 6:2 says "thou art snared with the words of thy mouth," and she was tying herself up in knots with her negative attitude. One day the Spirit of God gave me a phrase to help her see what she was doing to herself. "Before you speak, weigh the words that you speak and make sure that they have enough value to come out of your mouth." Candas received that word, and it changed her life.

If you want people to listen to you, make sure your words have value. A great way to do this is to speak the Word of God. Face it, no one is interested in hearing more philosophy or opinion. People are searching for truth. And we know that we can find the truth in God's Word.

> While we look not at the things which are seen, but at the things that are not seen: for the things which are seen are temporal; but the things which are not seen are eternal.

> 2 Corinthians 4:18

Maybe you have gotten the impression that by esteeming the situation that you will always choose what is "right" and refuse what is wrong. That is not correct. We choose what we *value* and refuse things of *lesser value.*

When I first became a pastor, there was a young man attending the church who loved God and felt he was called to preach. But he was facing financial hardship. It seemed that every time he turned around he was having money problems.

This was a particularly difficult problem for him because of his family situation. His father owned a very large and profitable business, and the young man knew that he could work for his father and make a lot of money, even though he did not believe that was what God wanted him to do.

Unfortunately he began to focus his attention on his circumstances, and he stopped looking at what God had called him to do. After a while he looked only at what his father could do for him. He decided to return to his hometown and the family business.

His wife called me some time later and asked me to pray for them. She told me that her husband had begun to drink alcohol quite heavily, both of them were smoking again, and they had gone back to what she referred to as their "old life." He was not preaching anymore, and their spiritual life was almost non-existent. She said the "old life" was not very good.

Do you see that it is possible to refuse what is good and choose what is bad? We need to realize that people make wrong choices. We can learn from their experiences so that we can avoid making similar mistakes.

I do a lot of preaching and teaching, and I notice the people who are listening, watching, hanging onto the teaching that I have for them. You can tell that the message is important to them. Because they have *chosen* to hear the message, they have *refused* the distractions that are present at any public gathering. They have made a quality decision.

Decision making is more than just having a good idea and "deciding" that accomplishing it would be nice. Decision making that really works, is the result of carefully weighing and balancing the choices presented to you, then, by following the scriptural principles of choosing and refusing, setting out quality priorities. Only then you will be able, by esteeming and valuing the Word of God, to discern what is bad, what is merely good, and what is best for you. And, like Mary of Bethany who chose to sit at Jesus' feet instead of being "cumbered about much serving" (Luke 10:40) as we will discuss later, you will *choose the good part.*

4

THE PROCESS OF "FORSAKING"

By faith he (Moses) forsook Egypt,

not fearing the wrath of the king.

Hebrews 11:27

Until this point we have been talking about the mental part of the decision. Now it is time to put your decision into motion. We are ready for the action steps.

It Is Time for Action

Those who *act* and those who just *think* they want to act will be separated at this point. In quality decision making, this is the point of defeat for those who only mentally assent to their decisions, plans, or goals. Many people have heard from God and said yes, but few get up and go.

The Bible says, "Many are called, but few are chosen" (Matt. 22:14). That means they do not act. But Paul said, "Forgetting those things which are behind, and reaching forth unto those things which are before, *I press toward the mark* for the prize of the high calling of God in Christ Jesus" (Phil. 3:13,14). He took action.

Mere Mental Assent

Many people have the greatest intentions in the world, but they never do anything. They have gone through the "head steps" of the process, but they never take any *action* to set the decision in motion. They complete three steps of a seven-step process, then wonder why things did not work out as they had planned.

A quality decision is more than mental assent or a good idea. If you decide to do something but take no action, *you have only made half a decision.* Most Christians *desire* to do the things of God, to follow Him and to do His will. They want to "get with the program." But if you spend all your time and effort in the mental realm, you will never accomplish anything.

God's solution for getting past mere mental assent is the fourth step of quality decision making, the process of learning how to "forsake." Forsake means not only to leave, but to leave something behind you.[5] This "leaving behind" is inherent in the process of quality decision making. You can talk about doing something, you can think about doing something, but nothing will happen until you leave the old things behind and start *doing* what you decided to do.

When Moses refused to be called son of Pharaoh's daughter, he made a firm mental decision. Then he came to the place where he had to act out physically what he had determined in his heart. He had to forsake Egypt and its "advantages."

Obstacles to Action

The devil will use any tool he can to hinder you: your background, your race, your relationships, your education or lack of it, your attitude, your fears. What obstacles are preventing you from acting on the ideas, dreams, and visions that God has planted in your heart? Let us examine some of the common obstructions to accomplishing your goals.

The Negative Power of Fear

Notice the Bible says that Moses left Egypt behind "without giving thought to the king's wrath" (Heb. 11:27).

He knew the king would be mad! Angry! Irate! Furious! Enraged! If a person ever had a chance to fear, Moses certainly did at this time.

Can you imagine what was going through Moses's mind when the time came to lead God's people out of Egypt? Until then everything had been theoretical, but now the reality of the situation was on him. If Moses actually took all those slaves from Egypt, the king would lose great wealth and the bulk of his work force. I am sure the devil told Moses, "Listen, boy, if the king ever catches you, you are done for. You have really messed up *big* this time!"

Fear Will Try To Stop You

Grab hold of this point: *unless you take charge, fear will stop you from acting.* It will render you ineffective. Fear of people and fear of failure has stopped many people from doing what God has asked them to do. Fear is the opposite of faith.

Fear comes with different faces. Sometimes we may be stopped by a silly feeling of embarrassment. Perhaps we have decided to exercise the gifts of the Spirit that the Lord has given us, to be "God's man of faith and power." Then when God says to lay hands on the sick, we are embarrassed. We desire to prophesy, but when God says, "Say this to the people," we respond by saying, "Lord, You know I can't do *that!*"

You Don't Mean Me, Lord?

Another obstacle to action is a sense of inadequacy, the feeling that we simply are not able to do the job. The story of Gideon found in the sixth chapter of Judges portrays a man who thought God had made a mistake in choosing him.

As Gideon hid from the Midianites, the angel of the Lord appeared and said, "The Lord is with thee, thou mighty man of valor" (Judg. 6:12). If Gideon heard the "mighty man of valor" part, he certainly did not appear to believe it. Instead he complained about the circumstances facing him and his people.

And the Lord looked upon him, and said, *Go in this thy might,* and thou shalt save Israel from the hands of the Midianites: *have I not sent thee?*

Judges 6:14

Next, Gideon spoke of how poor and insignificant he and his family were. He said that he was the most insignificant of the bunch!

His father had named him "Gideon," meaning a warrior.[6] But after his encounter with the angel of the Lord, and after Gideon had destroyed the altars of Baal his father had built, his father changed his name to "Jerubaal." That word means contending, fighting, or grappling against Baal.[7] Today we would say "devil fighter."

Did Gideon see himself as a man of valor, as a man with God-given might, as a devil fighter? Still not understanding the position that God had given him, Gideon "set out fleeces" to confirm God's word. His negative self-image hindered the plans of God, an obstacle he was finally able to overcome.

Moses had faced this same kind of obstacle. When God first commanded him to deliver the children of Israel out of Egypt, Moses replied, "Who am I, that I should go unto Pharaoh, and that I should bring forth the children of Israel out of Egypt?" (Ex. 3:11). God reassured Moses that He would be with him every step of the way, but Moses still hesitated. "O my Lord, I am not eloquent, neither heretofore, nor since thou hast spoken unto thy servant: but I am slow of speech, and of a slow tongue" (Ex. 4:10). In his *heart* the decision had already been made. He knew his desire was that God's children would be delivered from slavery. But when it came time to act, he was filled with doubt. He did not believe God could use someone like him with so many imperfections.

But the time came when Moses put all his excuses behind him. "Refusing" is a heart action; "forsaking" is a physical action. When Moses refused to be called the son of Pharaoh's daughter, he made the decision in his heart. But when he forsook Egypt, he took physical action. *And he took that physical action by faith.* He did not know much about where he was going. He just knew that God had instructed him to leave Egypt with the children of Israel. And he was going to *do it*, no matter what.

Have you ever felt that you were inferior, that your weaknesses and shortcomings made you unsuitable for God to use you? Gideon and Moses felt the same way. But look how God used them when they became willing to forsake the excuses of the past, to serve Him despite their shortcomings.

Past Failures

The devil will gladly remind you of your past failures. *Do you remember when you blew it?* the devil will ask you. And it is true, you have messed up before. The devil — if you let him — will beat you over the head. He will remind you of other mistakes and botches and messes you have made until you begin to feel that *you* are the failure, not just someone who has made some mistakes. Always remember that God does not make failures. He only creates winners. "For in Him we live, and move, and have our being" (Acts 17:28).

Giving Up Security

Many people have had to face a life-changing decision. It is difficult to deal with the obstacles of leaving the comforts of home, leaving the security of a particular town or a particular job. And many people have balanced things out and recognized that their lives would be better if they served the Lord. But when the time comes for action, they want the security of their "safety net."

After working with Kenneth Hagin Ministries for more than ten years, a time came to leave and begin another work. My wife and I had reached a point where we were beginning to be blessed financially after years of sacrifice. As we esteemed our situation, we had to deal with giving up financial security.

Do you have security aspects in your life that are interfering with what you know you are supposed to do? Health insurance — vacation pay — sick leave — retirement benefits? When it is time to act on your decision, that old flesh will jump up and holler and turn sideways on you. The decision you were considering seemed noble, but when the time to step out arrives, it is scary! I have been in situations where I knew what I should do; I had to act on the Word in my heart. But that did not make it easy. That is where the sheep are separated from the goats.

A number of years ago when I pastored, I knew the Lord was telling me that it was time to move our church to a new location. We had an option to renew the lease on our current building, and I thought that it was good business to exercise the option. That way I knew that at least we had a place to have services if nothing else opened up. I had been praying and waiting for direction as to the new location. And, at the same time, I was busy looking for a location.

I looked everywhere in the city. I had made the decision in my heart that wherever God opened the door we would go. But one day the Lord told me in prayer, *You haven't left yet!* That is when I realized that I was still hanging on to the old building.

Then God told me, "You are going to have to forsake it." You see, I had made the decision in my heart, but I had not been willing to give up the security of the lease. I was hanging on to a building instead of trusting God totally. This time I decided to trust God in finding us a new location no matter how or where He led. Acting in faith, I forsook the option to renew and told the owner of the building that we were moving. Then, and only then, God miraculously opened up a new location for us.

The Obstacle of Pride

Earlier I described some of my experiences as a young man when I had to choose between a big job promotion and going into full-time ministry. I gave up my job and went to Minnesota as Music and Youth Director of a church when I couldn't even read music. I knew God had called me, so I went. And God began to bless me and the ministry.

But there is more to the story. I almost let pride destroy the work that God had called me to do.

About six months after I moved, the pastor asked me to come to his house. When I arrived he said, "Will you come outside? I've got some big boulders and rocks in my yard, and I need some help moving them." I was glad to be of assistance, so I went outside and began moving rocks.

When he said boulders, he meant it! After working for several hours, I sat down to drink a glass of water while the pastor went into the house. A few minutes later he came out through the garage pushing a lawn mower and shoved it in front of me. "I want you to know, I consider it part of your job to mow my yard," he said.

At no time had we ever discussed yard work as part of my job description. I had never even entertained the thought. I had been hired as Music and Youth Director, and I was having some difficulty seeing the relationship between these two jobs. Too angry to speak, I began mowing the yard.

Have you ever mowed a yard when you were mad? The yard was next to a big four-lane highway, and there was a lot of noise from the trucks and cars going by. It was a good thing because I was talking to myself pretty loudly. Pushing that lawn mower as fast as I could, I said, "Lord, I didn't come up here to be a yard boy. I'm going to go in there and tell him what he can do with this job."

I'm out there a'huffing and a'puffing in that yard just as mad as I can be, when the Spirit of God very gently spoke to me. He said, *Son, do you love Me?* With my teeth clenched I responded, "Lord, You know I love You."

I kept on shoving that lawn mower around when, a few minutes later, I heard the Spirit of God the second time. *Son, do you love Me?* He asked.

"Well, Lord, You know I love You."

But I was *still* mad. As I continued to mow, the voice came again, *Son, do you really love Me?* This time it really touched my heart. I said, "Oh, Lord, You know I love You. I would walk to China and back to prove that I love You."

He then said, *You don't have to walk to China to prove you love Me, Buddy. Just walk across the yard and mow it!*

I knew then that I would do whatever it took to be the best Music and Youth Director possible — even if that included mowing lawns.

I am not saying that it was right for the pastor to take advantage of me. But there is an important lesson here. Since I was in the process of a quality decision to be in full-time ministry, I had to overcome any obstacles the devil would throw at me. This included my pride.

Sometimes we have noble and gallant ideas about what we believe that God wants us to do. We decide to pay whatever price is necessary to go wherever God wants us to go. But when faced with the reality of life, the menial and often subservient jobs, many people will give up. They are not willing to humble themselves to get the job done.

Follow Love

A large part of a noble and grand decision is going to be pretty ordinary, insignificant, and seemingly unimportant. Whether it is mowing yards, cleaning commodes, or straightening chairs, it has to be done. If your pride can stop you at this level, you have not made a quality decision. You have only mentally assented. Let me tell you, when you start following love, you will do many things you never thought you would ever do.

Part of my job with Kenneth Hagin Ministries was to hold Brother Hagin's coat and Bible, to open the car door, and to drive him home. I chose to follow love. I made a decision to overcome the obstacles and to do everything that was required.

When I made a decision to go with the man of God, that decision included carrying the coat, opening the door, and doing what was necessary. It is all part of the same decision.

Act — in Faith

Moses refused to consider the wrath of the king. He stayed in faith knowing that "without faith it is impossible to please Him" (Heb. 11:6). Unless you determine to overcome the obstacles to your faith, you will be defeated. But because you learn to *act* in faith, the blessings of God *will* come your way. Forsaking the fears and obstacles of the past, you will be separated from those who just sit and talk. You will become *a doer of the Word.*

5

The Power of Endurance

For he endured, as seeing Him who is invisible.

Hebrews 11:27

So what else do I have to do? you may be wondering. *How much more "quality" can this decision get?*

You carefully weighed the options by the process of esteeming. Then you refused the lesser alternative and chose the more positive one by conscientiously setting priorities. Surely *this* decision cannot fail! What do I have to do now other than sit and watch it happen?

You Are Part of an Elite Group

First, take a little time to congratulate yourself. The truth is most people have never gotten this far in their decision making. The flip side is, because you are now understanding the process of godly decision making and are beginning to put the process in motion, you can be sure the devil will now do everything he can to stop you. After all, if you know how to make one quality decision, then you can make another, and another, and another — decisions that will make a difference.

This is when the quality of endurance, that trait of "hanging in there until," becomes fundamental to reaching your goal.

Look Out When You Think No One Understands You

Satan wants to isolate you, to get you off on your own, to "cut you out of the herd."

You're one of a kind, he will tell you. *There is nobody else who has gone through a situation like yours.* Malarkey! He may change the words or the presentation, but he will always hand you the same old tricks. Do not let him tell you that you are the only one who has walked this path, or that nobody understands what you are going through. He knows if he can get you out there alone, all by yourself, you will eventually have a pity party. As soon as you see it coming, just think of it as garbage — because that is exactly what it is. The devil is just trying to set you up for a big fall.

Be "Hard As Steel"

The Greek word translated *endured* in the text we have been studying means to be strong, to be steadfast, to be patient.[8] This same sense of strength is implied in the English word *endure* which comes from the Latin meaning "to harden like steel."[9] (*Durable,* another word from the same root, means "long lasting, highly resistant to wear.")[10] The sixth step of the process, endurance, is the quality of remaining constant, staying with it, no matter what.

Determined To Win

Have you ever watched a boxing match where one of the fighters was hanging on the ropes? You could almost hear him saying to himself, "If I can just hang on until the bell rings." And that is exactly what you have to do. Hang in there — until you win!

"Wherefore seeing we also are compassed about with so great a cloud of witnesses, let us lay aside every weight, and the sin which doth so easily beset us, and let us run with *patience* the race that is set before us" (Heb. 12:1). The word translated *patience* in this scripture does not mean tolerance or forbearance. (For many years I confused the words *patience* and *longsuffering*. I thought *patience* meant you had to "grin and bear it.")

Running the race "with patience" does not mean to run with a calm, serene look on your face, not being concerned when another runner is trying to pass. It does not mean to sit around twiddling your thumbs. ("Just be patient, dear. Don't get so upset!") No! It means we are to run the race with determination, with perseverance, with endurance.[11]

We are in this race to win! We have made a decision, and we are in for the long haul. This race is not over until we are in the winner's circle! This is the attitude you must have.

Keep Your Eyes on God

"By faith Moses forsook Egypt, not fearing the wrath of the king for he endured as seeing Him who is invisible" (Heb. 11:27). Moses *endured* because he looked to God. The writer of Hebrews used an interesting phrase here: "seeing Him who is invisible." How can you see someone who is invisible? We would say today that Moses endured and overcame because he kept his eyes on the Lord. He was focused.

This is a key concept. *You must keep your eyes on the Lord.* As you keep your eyes on God, you will endure. Endurance is the quality of remaining constant, staying with it, no matter what. As you become consistent and steady, people will comment that they trust you and that they can count on you. But if you do not keep your eyes on the Lord, you will give in to fear.

The disciples saw Jesus walking on the water in the midst of a storm, and they cried out in fear. They thought they had seen a spirit. But Peter fixed his eyes on the Lord, and the next thing we know, Peter leaves the boat and starts walking on the water himself! (Matt. 14:25-29.) "But when he saw the wind boisterous, he was afraid; and beginning to sink, he cried, saying, Lord, save me" (Matt. 14:30). When Peter got his eyes on the circumstances, he was no longer "seeing Him who was invisible."

You Do Not Have To Go Under

If you have made a decision but have taken your eyes off Jesus, then this is a time to be *encouraged,* not discouraged — Jesus is going to reach out and take hold of you. Even if you falter in the middle of the "enduring" stage and it appears that you are sinking, just get your eyes back on Jesus. Make an adjustment, make a correction. *You do not have to sink anymore.* Certainly you do not have to sink all the way. Peter "began sinking," but he did not go under. Get your eyes back on the Lord, and He will pick you up. He did it for Peter, and He will do it for you, too.

Believe That God Will Keep His Promises

The law of faith is in operation when you are in the process of enduring. You may have set aside your dream for a time, but as you put your eyes on the Lord, then this "constant vision" will re-activate the law of faith and you will be right back on track.

Abraham learned about enduring. When he was still named Abram, God told him he would have so many descendants he would not be able to count them. (Gen. 15:2-5.) The problem was that he was seventy-five years old and he did not have any children! There were other complications, also. His wife was barren and could not have children (Gen. 11:30), and even if she had not been barren, she was now too old to have children!

Right then and right there *Abraham believed God.* But Sarah did not get pregnant. Not that year nor the next year nor the year after that. Abraham endured and kept on believing — for twenty-five years! (Gen. 21:1,5.) The Bible says Abraham:

> Who against hope believed in hope, that he might become the father of many nations, according to that which was spoken, so shall thy seed be. And being not weak in faith, he considered not his own body now dead, when he was about an hundred years old, neither yet the deadness of Sarah's womb: he staggered not at the promise of God through unbelief; but was strong in faith, giving glory to God; And being fully persuaded, that what He had promised, He was able also to perform.
>
> Romans 4:18-21

Do Not Look at the Circumstances

What an extraordinary description of the process of endurance. "Who against hope believed in hope." When God said, "Look now toward heaven, and tell (count) the stars, if thou be able to number them . . . so shall thy seed be" (Gen. 15:5), there was no earthly reason to believe that it would ever be true. But Abraham did not look at the circumstances. "He considered not his own body nor the deadness of Sarah's womb." If he had looked at those things, he would not have endured. Instead, he was fully persuaded that God was able to do what He promised He would do. "God, You said it, and that settles it!" He was *"strong in faith,"* so much so that God looked at it the same way He looks at righteousness (Rom. 4:22).

Give God the Glory Right Now

Abraham "was strong in faith, giving glory to God." When? After the baby was born? After God had come through with the answer? It is easy to give God glory when the promise is manifested, when we see it with our very own eyes. But Abraham started giving God the glory *when God gave him the promise.* He started thanking and praising God right away. And he endured for *twenty-five years.* Some of us get discouraged if our prayers are not answered in two weeks!

Dust Off Your Dream

Has God ever given you a dream, a vision and plan, that has caused you to be so excited that you were not able to sleep? But then the devil started chatting with you about "reality."

Why, there is no way you will ever get something like that done, that demon of discouragement will say to you. *That is too expensive. That is too complicated. Someone else will have to do that project. Besides, no one appreciates your hard work anyway!*

That God-given dream of yours started sinking as if it had concrete blocks tied to it. Admit it — you gave up on it. You began to question whether you had really heard from God in the first place! Maybe you thought it was just indigestion!

The time has come for you to dig in with the force of endurance and resurrect that dream. Endure. Remain constant, stay with it, hang in there — *no matter what!* Abraham did not have any hope, but he hoped anyway. Get your eyes off your circumstances, quit considering what your senses are telling you (and what your relatives are probably telling you, too), and start giving glory to God.

It is really true: God *is* able to perform that which He promises. And that is something to shout about!

6

KEEP DOING WHAT
YOU KNOW TO DO

Through faith he kept the passover,
and the sprinkling of blood, lest he that
destroyed the firstborn should touch them.

Hebrews 11:28

The sixth step to a quality decision is to *keep doing
what you already know to do.*

Staying in Faith

Until you have completed all seven steps of the
decision-making process, your goal is still not
achieved. A "dream house" begins as a dream. Later,
when we see the architect's drawings and the
blueprints, it is still not a house. And it is not a good
idea to try to live in it while it is under construction.

The decision you made, the one that started taking shape when you were esteeming, is a "faith project." That means you have to act by the rules of faith. And the key to a powerful faith life is getting God's Word in your heart, believing that Word, and acting on that Word.

Do Not Lose Your Perspective

In the old days people used to put "blinders" on horses so they would look straight ahead and not be distracted or spooked by things going on around them. Sometimes a new idea or a new goal rises up so big that we seem to have blinders on, too. Everything else is overshadowed. But don't do that! You do not want to block out everything you have learned before.

Maybe you think that is pretty self-evident. But, friend, it is not unusual to see a man or a woman get a good idea — maybe even a great idea — then go after that conviction with a fervor and intensity that excludes everything else. They seem to forget who they are and where they are. They lose sight of their former priorities — their family, friends, church, everything — then wonder why their lives are going downhill. That is crazy. You do not throw away the old. Instead you build upon those things. You do the things that have already been entrusted to you. *You keep doing what you already know to do.*

Do Not Ignore What Went Before

Be sure to distinguish between "doing what you know to do" and "forsaking the past." They are not the same.

When you reached the action part of the process in Step Four and started forsaking the past, you began to get rid of some things that plagued you in the past — things like poor self-image, fear, self-doubt, and pride. That process is hard work, and it is an on-going process. But you do not throw out *everything* you have learned in the past! I am not suggesting that you get amnesia! There are lots of things in your past that are good! And many of those things are things that you need to keep doing.

What is important about doing what you know to do? "Therefore to him that knoweth to do good, and doeth it not, to him it is sin" (James 4:17). Whatever is of sin is not from God. Certainly it is not faith.

The Passover and the sprinkling of the blood were not ancient history to Moses and the children of Israel. The sprinkling of the blood is what saved the lives of their firstborn. But God expected Moses to remember and observe the Passover events as a memorial to His delivering power. Moses might have turned it into a ritual, just a ceremony or a formality (like some church services today). But God *entrusted* this memorial to Moses who determined that it would be "kept."

Make It Happen

Why would God insist on this? He does not need a bunch of ceremonies for His own benefit. So why is it so important that Moses "kept" the Passover and the sprinkling of the blood?

The English word "kept" is a common word. (I "kept" the cottage cheese in the refrigerator, and I "kept" the dog in the backyard!) But the Greek word that is translated "kept" here is a root word, one that does not come from any other word in the language. Used 565 times in the New Testament, its meaning is strong and powerful. Usually translated as "to do" or "to make," the sense of the word is *to cause something to happen.*[12] It means to produce, to perform, and to accomplish what you have purposed to do. "We *will* keep the Passover," Moses was saying, "even if we are leaving town and nobody knows us where we are going! And we are going to do it because God told us to do it!" It *would* be produced, performed, and accomplished. He determined that he would *make it happen!*

Moses determined that the Passover would be "kept." One way to tell if a decision is a "quality decision" is to look at how long it lasts. So it is interesting to see that Jesus, preparing for the "Last Supper,"[13] said to His disciples, "Go into the city to such a man, and say unto him, The Master saith, My time is at hand; I will *keep the passover* at thy house with my disciples" (Matt. 26:18). The decision Moses made was definitely a quality decision.

Stop the Devil From Wrecking Your Decisions

There was another reason for keeping the Passover and the sprinkling of the blood. Notice the rest of

Hebrews 11:28: "...Lest he that destroyed the firstborn should touch them." This is a direct reference to Satan, the thief "who comes to steal, to kill and to destroy" (John 10:10).

By continuing to do what you know to do — no matter what — you block the devil from destroying you and your family, your money, and your possessions. You deny him any legal right to interfere in your life. On the other hand, if you become lazy, preoccupied, or just plain rebellious, and stop doing what you know to do, the devil has an open door to tear you up. You have let down the barrier so the enemy can come in and counteract the decision that you have made. This is a biblical principle.

Samson Lets Down His Guard

The story of Samson (Judg. 13-16) is a little fuzzy to many Christians. Lots of people remember the part about Samson's slaying Philistines with the jawbone of a donkey, and everybody remembers Delilah, the woman hired by the Philistines to find out from Samson the source of his strength and power.

What many people do not know is that Samson was one of Israel's "judges" recorded in the Book of Judges. Chosen by God before he was born, Samson was dedicated to the Lord by his parents with the "vow of a Nazirite" and served as judge for twenty years. The sorry end of his life is an illustration of the consequences of not doing what you already know to do.

God Knows Us Even Before We Are Born

Specific laws applied to Nazirites, young men who were especially "dedicated to God." They could not be "unclean" in any way, and were forbidden, among other things, to eat or drink anything that came from grapes (especially wine) or to cut their hair. So when Samson got drunk at Delilah's house and told her that the secret of his strength was in his long hair, we see a Nazirite in a *very* bad position.

You Are Responsible for Whatever Knowledge You Have

The story of Samson is not some absurd tale of a "Superman" who leaks the secret of his "Super

Strength." Samson knew the sanctity of his vows to God. He knew that the source of his famous strength lay not in his hair but in his special relationship with God and his special vow of purity.

In fact, Samson probably had more knowledge of these matters than anyone else. He had served in the position of judge, the "Deliverer of God's People," for his entire adult life. *And God held him accountable for this knowledge.*

God had given Samson great responsibilities and had rewarded him with supernatural power and abilities. But Samson stopped doing what he knew to do. Is it any wonder that he was enslaved and blinded by the very enemy he had been called to overcome?

Do you know what the Bible says about tithing? Have you ever heard a sermon or listened to a teaching tape about tithing? If you *know* the biblical principles of tithing, then you must tithe if you expect to receive the blessings and benefits due to tithers. And just because you have made a quality decision to set in motion a plan that God has given you does not make you exempt from doing what you already know to do.

"Be Doers of the Word"

James made a simple statement. "Be ye doers of the Word, and not hearers only, *deceiving your own selves*" (James 1:22). Failing to do what you know to do has a direct — and dramatic — impact on the results you want to have.

If a person does not keep doing what he knows to do — if he stops walking in the knowledge that he has — he immediately opens the door for the enemy to come in. He has no right to blame someone else; he is doing it to himself. You are *required* to walk in the light that you have received. And if you do not, you defeat yourself.

The Bible teaches us that love is the foundation of our relationships with other people — our parents, our children, our spouse, our friends, even our enemies. You probably know that you must give your mate a certain amount of attention or problems are going to arise. If you know this, then you must do it. This is part of walking in love.

Many a man has blamed someone else for the destruction of his marriage. "Yeah, if so-and-so hadn't been paying attention to her, I wouldn't have lost her." Malarkey! If you know to do something in your marriage and you do not do it, the relationship will deteriorate. Eventually it will be destroyed. That person has no one to blame but himself.

If a person is able-bodied, he knows he has to work. What is my advice to someone who can work and does not? Simple. Get a job! Do not just sit there saying, "I hope God does something about this mess I am in."

Start Now

Be a doer of the Word. You can start right now by applying the principles you are learning about decision making. Start now — this moment — present tense! Moses kept doing what he knew to do. He was the leader, the boss, the big man. There was no one to tell him that he had to keep the Passover and the sprinkling of the blood. But he refused to open the door to the devil. You, too, will shut the door in the devil's face as you keep doing what you already know to do!

7

~~~

PASSING THROUGH

By faith they passed through

the Red sea as by dry land.

Hebrews 11:29

We have now come to the seventh and last step in the making of a quality decision. We are now ready to *pass through*. This is the part that we looked forward to when we made the decision in the very beginning, when it was just a good idea.

First you esteem the situation. Then you refuse. Then you choose. Then you forsake. Then you endure. Then you keep doing what you know to do. Now you are ready to pass through! It is all part of the same decision.

Moses knew that he had been chosen by God, that he was the deliverer. He made a quality decision

when he said, "I'm going with it — I'll do it, Lord."
But look at the obstacles that he faced in the process.

Unwavering Determination

Smith Wigglesworth was a mighty man of God.
There were confirmations of numerous healings that
occurred both privately and in his public meetings.
People were actually raised from the dead.

Yet Wigglesworth was afflicted with kidney stones
in the latter part of his life. Doctors examined him
and recommended surgery. But he refused. He made
a *decision* that no man would ever operate upon him,
and that if he were to be healed, God would have to
perform the operation.

He chose to forsake the natural for the
supernatural. Realize that this man often ministered
three or four times a day. Many times while in the
very midst of ministering to the sick, he would be
attacked with the pain of another kidney stone. He
would tell the congregation to keep praising the Lord
and would go to a side room to pass one of those
kidney stones, then return to continue ministering to

the sick. You can imagine the excruciating pain that he must have gone through.

Smith Wigglesworth waited for seven years, but he died without kidney stones! How long do you wait for the manifestation? How long do you wait for the fullness of what you desire of God? As long as it takes. As long as necessary. Until you pass through.

Know That God Is With You

We may be deceived into believing that crossing the Red Sea was easy for Moses. After all, he was a mighty man of faith. But, also, we know the end of the story! We know that the Sea is going to open up and everything is going to work out.

But when you are standing at the edge of *your* Red Sea, when you have done everything that you know to do and the circumstances look impossible, the temptation to quit will never be stronger.

But what a wonderful promise God has given us:

When thou passest through the waters, I will be with thee; and through the rivers, they shall not overflow thee: when thou walkest through the fire, thou shalt not be burned; neither shall the flame kindle up on

thee. For I am the Lord thy God, the Holy One of
Israel, thy Saviour . . . .

Isaiah 43:2,3

The Effect of Other Decisions

Too many people believe that when they first
made a commitment to a decision that somehow it is
a done deal. No, that is just the beginning. They have
just started. Now they must endure, and they must
keep doing what God has told them to do.

Moses had to keep observing ordinances that God
had set in motion. He could not lay them aside. Why?
Because he knew that if he did that the enemy would
try to steal from him. A new decision is not made in a
vacuum. When you are in the process of bringing one
decision to completion, there will be other decisions
to make along the way. And those decisions must be
based on their own merits at the time they are made.
But future decisions may very well affect major
decisions already in process. The new choices must be
esteemed. You must judge, balance, weigh, measure,
and account their importance.

God Is on Your Side

My father was a gambler. All during the years I was growing up I heard, "The odds are against you." But I want you to know that if God is for you, who can possibly stand against you? *How am I going to make it, you wonder?* By "looking unto Jesus the author and finisher of our faith; who for the joy that was set before him endured the cross, despising the shame, and is set down at the right hand of the throne of God" (Heb. 12:2). You are able to pass through by "seeing Him who is invisible."

8

GODLY EXAMPLES

…Verily, verily, I say unto you, The Son can
do nothing of himself, but what he seeth the
Father do: for what things soever he doeth,
these also doeth the Son likewise.

John 5:19

God gave us the pattern for making quality
decisions. (Heb. 11:24-29.) Now let's look at some
examples in the Bible of the pattern in action. If you
can see the pattern, you can understand the pattern.
But until you put the pattern in *action,* your decisions
will lack the quality that God desires for your life.
"What doth it profit, my brethren, though a man say
he hath faith, and have not works?" (James 2:14).

Making Short-Term and Long-Term Quality Decisions

As I have said, this decision-making process applies to natural as well as spiritual decisions. It also applies to short-term and long-term decisions.

For an example of a short-term decision (we might call it an "everyday" decision), let's look at a familiar Bible story.

> Now it came to pass, as [Jesus and the disciples] went, that [Jesus] entered into a certain village: and a certain woman named Martha received him into her house. And she had a sister called Mary, which also sat at Jesus' feet, and heard his word. But Martha was cumbered about much serving, and came to him, and said, Lord, dost thou not care that my sister hath left me to serve alone? bid her therefore that she help me. And Jesus answered and said unto her, Martha, Martha, thou art careful and troubled about many things: But one thing is needful: and Mary hath chosen that good part, which shall not be taken away from her.
>
> Luke 10:38-42

This account by Luke is not a parable. The writer is telling us about a "certain woman" and her sister, a real story about real people. Contained in these few verses are the kernels of the decision-making process as demonstrated by Mary.

It was an honor to prepare a meal for the Master. How excited Mary and Martha must have been when word came that Jesus and His disciples were coming to their village. And even more exciting, He was coming to *their* home. This wasn't a politician coming by for a ten-minute "photo opportunity." The Rabbi, Himself, was coming to their house where He would teach, have a meal, and probably spend the night.

The Pressures of Everyday Life

Imagine what it is like to invite guests to your home for dinner. You spend time planning the meal and buying the food. You make sure the house is clean. And of course, you make sure that the food is prepared just the right way.

To put this in perspective, think about the pressure if you were responsible for preparing Thanksgiving dinner for 20 or 25 people. Perhaps you plan wisely and prepare much of the dinner in advance. Still, think of the work involved just to get a hot meal on the table for that many people. Now imagine preparing that same dinner for a celebrity, such as the governor of the state. Now we are getting an idea of the responsibility and pressure that Martha was feeling. This was a *big deal!* "Martha was distracted with much serving" (v. 40 NKJV).

Jesus didn't care what was on the menu that night. His time on earth was drawing to an end. He must have been thinking how little time was left and how much still needed to be done. Every opportunity to prepare His disciples for what lay ahead must have been important to Him. But the meal was important to *Martha.* It was a matter of pride. What would her friends and neighbors say if she didn't prepare a big meal for Jesus? She would never hear the end of it!

Choosing Between the Natural and the Eternal

We have no reason to believe that Mary was inconsiderate or rude to her sister Martha. Nor is there anything in the story to suggest that Mary was lazy or not able to help. But examining the situation in the light of quality decision making, we can see that Mary *esteemed* the situation differently than her sister did. She knew she had to choose between her obligation to Martha and listening to what Jesus had to say.

Distractions and Anxieties

Mary *refused* to let the care of feeding the guests keep her from the Word. In verse 41, the word "careful" is translated from the Greek word *merimnao*. This same word is translated "thought" in Matthew 6:25: "(therefore I say unto you, take no *thought* for your life, what ye shall eat, or what ye shall drink) and in Matthew 6:28, (why take ye *thought* for raiment)."

In Philippians 4:6 *merimnao* is translated as "careful." "Be *careful* for nothing; but in every thing by prayer and supplication with thanksgiving let your requests be made known unto God." And 1 Peter 5:7 uses the word *merimnao* as "care" "(casting all your care upon him [God]; for he careth for you)."[14]

In each of these verses the sense of the word *merimnao* is "to be anxious, to have a distracting care." Are there times when distractions or anxiety

come between you and Jesus? But the Word says
"Mary hath *chosen* that good part" (Luke 10:42). She
esteemed the situation, *refused* the distracting cares of
preparing the meal, and *chose* to sit at the feet of the
Master. Having made her decision, she *forsook* her
obligations as a hostess and sat with the guests to
listen to what Jesus had to say.

Opportunities To Give Up

Even though Mary's decision was short-term,
there was still an element of *endurance* in the process.
We can imagine that Martha had communicated her
feelings to Mary long before she interrupted the
Messiah. It probably started with a few whispered
comments, then stares and glares as Mary ignored the
kitchen and sat down in the living room. Perhaps
Martha banged a few pots and pans to remind her
sister that there was still work to do. The important
thing to note is that Mary had a number of chances
to change her mind. You can be sure that you, too,
will have opportunities to back away from any quality
decision that you make.

Despite the pressure from her sister and from others who were involved with the cooking, *Mary kept doing what she knew to do.* She knew that Jesus' words were important. She kept listening.

And can there be any question that Mary *passed through*? Jesus said "Mary hath chosen that good part, which shall not be taken away from her" (v. 42). The choice Mary made had eternal value and results.

Long-Term Decisions

The quality of your life will be determined by the quality of your daily decisions. Nevertheless, there are still decisions to make that will be major turning points. These "long-term decisions" clearly should be subjected to God's pattern for quality decisions.

Paul's Ministry Decision

For to me to live is Christ, and to die is gain. But if I live in the flesh, this is the fruit of my labour: yet what I shall choose I wot not.

For I am in a strait betwixt two, having a desire to depart, and to be with Christ; which is far better: Nevertheless to abide in the flesh is more needful for you.

And having this confidence, I know that I shall abide
and continue with you all for your furtherance and
joy of faith; That your rejoicing may be more
abundant in Jesus Christ for me by my coming to
you again.

Philippians 1:21-26

Paul was called by God through Jesus Christ to be
an apostle. (1 Cor. 1:1; Gal. 1:1.) He was saved
following a personal confrontation with Jesus whom
he had persecuted. (Acts 9:3-6.) He had visions and
revelations from the Lord. He was caught up into
heaven and heard things he was not allowed to reveal.
(2 Cor. 12:1-4.) Was it any wonder that he looked
forward to departing this earth to be present with
God the Father, the Son, and the Holy Spirit?

Appointment With Death

Many people believe that a person dies when "his
time has come." (Some of these people are Christians
who like to quote Hebrews 9:27: "It is appointed to
men once to die, but after this the judgment.")

Someone I knew liked to tell a story about himself.
One day he was working on a scaffold on a

construction site. A man next to him was being careless, and the man I knew told him to be careful.

"Oh, when it's time for me to go, then I'll go, and not before," said the man.

The man I knew (not a godly man) grabbed the careless man by his leg and held him over the edge of the scaffold. "Do you believe this is the time?" he asked!

I remember another story about a fellow who wanted his friend to go with him for a ride in a small plane.

"You're not afraid, are you?" taunted the man. "You're not going to die unless it's your time."

"That's not what I'm worried about," said his friend. "I'm afraid it might be *your* time!"

These stories show us that each of us clearly has a choice in the appointment with death. We can even set the appointment by violating one of the natural laws. For example if you violate the law of gravity by jumping off a cliff, you may very well be setting an appointment for death!

Many have been confused about the scriptural account of the martyrs that is set out in Hebrews 11:36-37:

> [They] had trial of cruel mockings and scourgings, yea, moreover of bonds and imprisonment: they were stoned, they were sawn asunder, were tempted, were slain with the sword.

But note that these people, immortalized as great men of faith, had a *choice* regarding the matter of their deaths. Others described in the same passage ". . . through faith subdued kingdoms, wrought righteousness, obtained promises, stopped the mouths of lions, quenched the violence of fire, escaped the edge of the sword" (Heb. 11:33,34).

What was the difference between these two groups? Those who were martyred ". . . were tortured, *not accepting deliverance; that they might obtain a* better resurrection" (Heb. 11:35). The implication is clear: Each of them could have accepted the deliverance of the Lord. Each made a clear choice to accept the form of death they received.

In the same manner Paul knew that he could if he desired go on to be with the Lord, or he could remain for the benefit of the believers. He made a quality decision with long-term effects to remain and continue in his ministry for our "furtherance and joy of faith." Thank God that Paul made that decision. He esteemed the value of the work as superior to the joy of going home to heaven. He forsook the desire to end the suffering and endured the hardships of prison continuing in his good work. Is there any question that he passed through receiving the approval of God Himself? A quality decision with long-term effects.

By following these biblical examples and by observing the pattern in other places in the Word of God, you will strengthen your own resolve to make the kinds of decisions that will have long-lasting and positive results in your life.

9

An Invitation and a Dare

Through faith we understand that
the worlds were framed by the word of God,
so that things which are seen were not
made of things which do appear.

Hebrews 11:3

God loved His servant Moses. And He loves His children who are called by His name. You are in the family. God will provide the money, the tools, the equipment, the knowledge, anything that you need. God will protect you and deliver you from the snares of the enemy.

When Moses came to the Red Sea, he could only see two things — the water and the enemy! A rock and a hard place! You know the feeling because you have been there.

But, friend, the seas will part! The tide will roll back for you, too.

It does not matter how big the waves look.

It does not matter how big the army coming against you may seem.

It does not matter what the numbers look like.

It does not matter what the reports say.

It does not matter what the odds are.

It does not matter what the statistics look like.

God has given you a pattern for decision making to follow.

You have learned to pray over the ideas that come to your mind and to esteem and value them.

You know to refuse those things that distract you from the place God wants you to go and to choose only those things that cause you to progress.

You see the importance of setting priorities and avoiding distractions.

By the process of forsaking, you have learned how to overcome obstacles and fears that have held you in bondage.

You hold fast to your decision by endurance.

You obstruct the power of the devil by doing the things you know to do, by being a doer of the Word.

Study these principles. Read and re-read them until you have committed them to memory. Ask trusted friends to hold you accountable. Then get ready for the fruits of quality decisions. As you follow these biblical principles, you will find yourself doing what God has called you to do. You will begin walking in God's perfect will. And you will experience the blessing of receiving the desires of your heart. You have passed through! Give God the glory.

ENDNOTES

1 *Webster's New World Dictionary*, 3d College Ed., based on "esteem."

2 James Strong, "Greek Dictionary of the New Testament," in *Strong's Exhaustive Concordance of the Bible* (Nashville: Abingdon, 1890), p. 35, #2233.

3 W. E. Vine, *Expository Dictionary of Biblical Words* (Nashville: Thomas Nelson Publishers, 1985), p. 517.

4 W. E. Vine, *Expository Dictionary of Biblical Words* (Nashville: Thomas Nelson Publishers, 1985), p. 100.

5 James Strong, "Greek Dictionary of the New Testament," in *Strong's Exhaustive Concordance of the Bible* (Nashville: Abingdon, 1890), #1439.

6 James Strong, "Hebrew and Chaldee Dictionary of the Old Testament," in *Strong's Exhaustive Concordance of the Bible* (Nashville: Abingdon, 1890), p. 26, #1440.

7 James Strong, "Hebrew and Chaldee Dictionary of the Old Testament," in *Strong's Exhaustive Concordance of the Bible* (Nashville: Abingdon, 1890), pp. 22, 52, and 108, ##1168, 3378, and 7378.

8 James Strong, "Greek Dictionary of the New Testament," in *Strong's Exhaustive Concordance of the Bible* (Nashville: Abingdon, 1890), p. 39, #2594; W. E. Vine, Expository Dictionary of Biblical Words (Nashville: Thomas Nelson Publishers, 1985), p. 200.

9 *Webster's New World Dictionary of American English,* Third College Edition, (New York: Prentice Hall, 1994), p. 449.

10 *Webster's New World Dictionary of American English,* Third College Edition, (New York: Prentice Hall, 1994), p. 422.

11 James Strong, "Greek Dictionary of the New Testament," in *Strong's Exhaustive Concordance of the Bible* (Nashville: Abingdon, 1890), p. 74, #5281; W. E. Vine, *Expository Dictionary of Biblical Words* (Nashville: Thomas Nelson Publishers, 1985), p. 462.

12 James Strong, "Greek Dictionary of the New Testament," in *Strong's Exhaustive Concordance of the Bible* (Nashville: Abingdon, 1890) p. 59, #4160; W. E. Vine, *Expository Dictionary of New Testament Words* (Nashville: Thomas Nelson Publishers, 1985), p. 340.

13 Dr. Frank Charles Thompson refers to this gathering as "The Last Passover," *Thompson Chain-Reference Bible,* New Testament, p. 32.

14 James Strong, *Strong's Exhaustive Concordance of the Bible* (Nashville: Regal Publishers, Inc.), p. 47, #3309.

Prayer of Salvation

God loves you—no matter who you are, no matter what your past. God loves you so much that He gave His one and only begotten Son for you. The Bible tells us that "…whoever believes in him shall not perish but have eternal life" (John 3:16 NIV). Jesus laid down His life and rose again so that we could spend eternity with Him in heaven and experience His absolute best on earth. If you would like to receive Jesus into your life, say the following prayer out loud and mean it from your heart.

Heavenly Father, I come to You admitting that I am a sinner. Right now, I choose to turn away from sin, and I ask You to cleanse me of all unrighteousness. I believe that Your Son, Jesus, died on the cross to take away my sins. I also believe that He rose again from the dead so that I might be forgiven of my sins and made righteous through faith in Him. I call upon the name of Jesus Christ to be the Savior and Lord of my life. Jesus, I choose to follow You and ask that You fill me with the power of the Holy Spirit. I declare that right now I am a child of God. I am free from sin and full of the righteousness of God. I am saved in Jesus' name. Amen.

If you prayed this prayer to receive Jesus Christ as your Savior for the first time, please contact us on the Web at **www.harrisonhouse.com** to receive a free book.

Or you may write to us at
Harrison House
P.O. Box 35035
Tulsa, Oklahoma 74153

ABOUT THE AUTHOR
Dr. Doyle "Buddy" Harrison

"By discipline and training you will receive more; and by being faithful and obedient, God will impart even more, so that you can fulfill the leadership position God has called you to."

—Buddy Harrison

Buddy Harrison, along with his wife, Pat, were Co-Founders of Faith Christian Fellowship International Church. He served as President of the organization from 1978 until he went home to be with the Lord on November 28, 1998. The Lord instructed Buddy to be a Pastor to Pastors and Ministers, providing guidance for them in the spiritual and natural realms. FCF International is in relationship with more than 1000 churches and 2000 ministers globally. Its programs include: Credentialing for ministers, Affiliation and Association of Churches, Strategic Planning, Family Care Center, Legal Advice, Accounting Consultation, On-site Management Consultation, Stewardship Services, and International Mission Program. It partners with The Life Link for humanitarian outreach. Dr. Harrison strongly believed in the value of covenant relationships and walking under authority, and he set the example for the FCF family. Today under the leadership of Pat Harrison, FCF continues

www.harrisonhouse.com

Fast. Easy. Convenient!

◆ New Book Information
◆ Look Inside the Book
◆ Press Releases
◆ Bestsellers

◆ Free E-News
◆ Author Biographies
◆ Upcoming Books
◆ Share Your Testimony

For the latest in book news and author information, please visit us on the Web at www.harrisonhouse.com. Get up-to-date pictures and details on all our powerful and life-changing products. Sign up for our e-mail newsletter, *Friends of the House,* and receive free monthly information on our authors and products including testimonials, author announcements, and more!

Harrison House—
Books That Bring Hope, Books That Bring Change

THE HARRISON HOUSE VISION

Proclaiming the truth and the power
Of the Gospel of Jesus Christ
With excellence;

Challenging Christians to
Live victoriously,
Grow spiritually,
Know God intimately.

to foster solid covenant relationships around the world among its ministers and churches.

As the Co-Founder and Chairman of Harrison House Publishers, Buddy obeyed God's vision to provide ministers a vehicle by which to put their message into print. Harrison House has become the largest Charismatic book publisher, with markets in more than 180 countries and publishing translations in 49 languages.

Buddy Harrison successfully incorporated his knowledge and skills of the corporate world with the Lord's calling on his life. As an anointed teacher and astute businessman, he traveled the world sharing these steps-to-success and favor.

To contact Mrs. Pat Harrison please write to:

Faith Christian Fellowship • International Church, Inc.
P.O. Box 35443 • Tulsa, OK 74153-0443
918-492-5800 • Web site: **www.fcf.org**

OTHER BOOKS BY BUDDY HARRISON

God's Banking System
Praying for the Impossible